"NO PARENT CAN CHILD-PROOF THE WORLD, A PARENT'S JOB IS TO WORLD-PROOF THE CHILD"

Doug Flanders

Parenting: From A Child's Perspective

TABLE OF CONTENTS

You Are The First Teacher/Example.....................Pages 5-9

Every Child Is Different ....Pages 10-13

Hear Us(Children) Out ....Pages 14-17

You Are Not Your Child.....................................Pages 18-22

Impact Of Family Dynamics On Children ....Pages 23-28

Go The Distance..Pages 29-32

Use Impactful Discipline....................................Pages 33-35

BE THERE...Pages 36-41

Instill A High Level Of Self-Esteem In Your Child.....Pages 42-48

Hindering Parenting Behaviors............................Pages 49-56

Ending Thoughts & Ideas....................................Pages 57-59

Reason For Writing...Pages 60-61

About The Author...Pages 62-64

Parenting: From A Child's Perspective

Per·spec·tive
/pər^ˈspektiv/

A Particular Attitude Toward Or Way Of Regarding

Something; A Point Of View, Way Of Thinking

SYN: Outlook, Viewpoint, Stance

Parenting: From A Child's Perspective

PERSPECTIVE

When you saw the front of the book, what were your thoughts? Did you think the father was berating and being rude to his son? How do you know the son didn't do something that could've cost him his life, and the dad wants him to understand how much he loves him as well as how important his choices are? There is no right or wrong answer in your responses, there is only your *Perspective.* In this book, I discuss my perspective on parenting and what we as children need from our parents, without trying to teach parents how to be parents. The following are stories and learning points not just from my life, but also from the lives of other children to help share a different perspective with you the reader.

You Are The First Teacher & Example

TWO SONS

There Were Twin Boys Raised By An Alcoholic

Abusive Father

One Grew Up To Be An Alcoholic

And Asked What Happened He Said

"I Watched My Father"

The Other Son Grew Up To Never Drink A Single Time

And When Asked Why He Said

"I Watched My Father"

Two **Perspectives**, Same Situation

You Can Even Replace The Alcoholic Abusive Father

For **Something Positive**

The TWO SONS Can Still Find Their Own Path In Life

With One Of Those Paths Being Negative Possibly.

As A Parent, Children Take In Everything You Do

Consciously And Subconsciously

Parenting: From A Child's Perspective

<u>MY FATHER'S EXAMPLE</u>

It was February of 2017 and Valentine's Day was approaching. At that time I had a girlfriend and it was going to be my first Valentine's Day; I never once thought, "what am I going to do?" A few days before I had got everything I needed to get, and on top of that I and made sure everything was 100% confirmed or available before that day. During the day when she went to class she received a poem I had given to her professor to give to her when she got there. I had left a card in her room for when she got back to her room with her favorite candy. Next in line was later on that night and we went out to a Painting With A Twist, and then after that was the grand finale. I had set the room up already before we went out and got my friend to light the candles on the way back from the Painting With A Twist. We finally got to my room and she opens the door and starts crying; it was gifts, candles lit, roses on the ground, and a dozen roses I had given her, more cards, and the stuffed animal she wanted. She had posted it on social media and so did I, and that's when this story comes full circle. Of course you have the "I need a man like that" sayings, but hearing the responses from other men was more impactful to me. Men were direct messaging as well as asking me in person where did that come from, why and how did I know to do that. While I was doing it, I didn't think much of it, but then I quickly realized it was just instinct from watching my dad care for my mother. I took a step back and I realized it was all the things my dad does for my mother (with my own personalized twist of course). My father showed me that example, how to cater, and pour into my partner and even though my and my father never actually spoke on how to do those type of things, he didn't need to because he showed and shows me daily with my mom.

Parenting: From A Child's Perspective

<u>You Are The First Teacher/Example</u>

Point To Ponder: Children Copy & Mirror Actions Better Than They Listen. Being An *Example* Is More Important Than Telling Someone What To Do. A lot of people who haven't been given the correct *advice*, in result follow in *example* of the wrong things.

Questions To Consider: Are You Yourself The Standard You Want For Your Child? If You Couldn't Speak, What Would Your Child Learn From Or How Would Your Child Benefit From Your Actions?

Every

Child Is

Different

Parenting: From A Child's Perspective

We as human beings have habits, certain ways that we react or do things, that have become second nature to us. For instance, every morning when I wake up I stretch, drink water, do a small workout, and read. That didn't just happen, over time that became a habit. Years ago, one of my father's habits was yelling at us (I have the greatest father in the world and he has grown in ways unimaginable and I want to be the father he is to his kids). Going back to habits, we don't normally change them, so as parents it is important to make sure that your parenting habits are positive and fitting for each child. One of the beautiful things in this world is that everyone thinks differently. With that being said, the way you parent each child will be received in a different way. In the past, me and one of my sisters could have done something wrong and got caught, and as a result we were both to be disciplined. At that time, as previously stated, my dad was a yeller. When my dad yelled at me it didn't phase me whatsoever and I would take heed to what he was saying. My sister, on the other hand, may be getting yelled at in the same tone or manner, and would completely shut down and cry so his teachings/discipline wouldn't reach her. The only thing she saw was her father and protector, yelling at her and felt bad about it. In no way shape or form am I saying not to discipline your children, because believe me we needed it and all children do. We mess up, do wrong, and are disobedient at times, but at the same time also realize that the purpose of discipline is to change behavior. My point here is to get parents to realize that the same way every child is different, you may possibly have to alter the way that you parent each child.

Parenting: From A Child's Perspective

<u>Every Child Is Different</u>

Point To Ponder: No Two People Are Alike; The Way People Recieve Things Are Different As Well As The Way We React Based On Our Emotions. This Understanding Must Be Taken Into Consideration Not Only While Parenting, But With Any Form Of Relationship.

Questions To Consider: Has There Ever Been A Time In Your Life Where The Same Thing Was Said To You And Another Person & You Both Took It Differently?

HEAR US

OUT

Parenting: From A Child's Perspective

Everyone in this world has a voice, you can even learn from people who have failed and speak wrongly. You can always learn something when someone speaks, whether it will help you or not is debatable. One thing that will help improve the parent-child connection is your child having a voice in the home. I didn't say the child is allowed to disrespect the parent at will, but the child should have a voice. You would be surprised at the amount of children who don't speak up out of fear or because they were never given that right growing up. One of the most important things in the world is constructive criticism and feedback. There could be something you do that you think your child likes, but in reality they hate and because they feel like they don't have a voice they won't say anything. There should be many conversations to figure out what your child is into, what they like, dislike and want to do with their lives. If your child can't tell you or feel like they can speak to you when something goes right, you can completely forget about them telling you about something bad happening. Parents have to give their child a safe space to be able to speak without being or feeling judge so that those conversations can take place. Giving children a voice benefits self esteem and their self worth. By giving children a voice in the home through choice, opinion, feelings and emotions they will learn and develop that they are important and valued. If something was to take place that hurt a child, they should feel comfortable enough to tell the parent. The parent make make the communication so that this is an okay thing to do. There are people who don't speak on certain things because of fear and how they'll be received, your child should not have to worry about that.

Parenting: From A Child's Perspective

<u>HEAR US OUT</u>

Point To Ponder: If The Child Never Has A Voice In The Home, How Is He/She Suppose To Learn To Speak Up For Themselves.

Questions To Consider: Would You Yourself Seek Out Someone To Share Information With That You Don't Feel Secure With?

You Are

Not Your

Child

Parenting: From A Child's Perspective

During the summer between ninth and 10th grade, I spent a lot of time at the YMCA "working out" to get better at basketball. I would normally go in the morning, and every morning there was a father there with his son, training him very hard. The father's goal was to get his son into the NBA, so he wasn't necessarily hard on him he was training him the way he needed to be trained in order for that goal to be obtained. Even at that time it was very clear to me and others, that playing basketball was not something that the son really wanted to do. He was never responsive, and never smiled, showed emotion, or passion; it was awkward actually. After a few years went by, I was a sophomore in college at this time, I had came home from school and seen the young man at a Wawa near my house. I asked him if he still plays basketball or where he plays basketball at now and he told me that he doesn't play anymore. He even told me that he had got scholarships to go to different schools on different

Parenting: From A Child's Perspective

levels. He chose not to go simply because of the fact that that was never really something that he wanted to do, but it was something that his father wanted to do. We talked for a little bit and about 5 minutes in he told me that his father had been a really good basketball player when he was in high school. He told me about how his father broke his leg in the midst of his senior season and ended up losing his scholarships. So when his son was born, he wanted his son to play in the NBA and there's nothing wrong with that at all. The thing his father didn't take into account was whether or not his son wanted to play or even enjoyed basketball at all. It doesn't have to be just basketball though, it could be trying to choose your child's career path in life. It could be shaming all areas except one so your child feels obligated to follow in suit in what YOU the parent wants. In some cases it is actually a good thing to do to get them started early on but you also want to make sure that they like it, we hear it all the time about the parents

Parenting: From A Child's Perspective

try to force their kids to go to certain universities or choose certain paths because that's where they think is best. As a parent, your child needs you to help them grow in the areas they are trying to grow in and best see fit for themselves. Don't parent the child based off of who you wanted to become or what you want them to become. Make sure your child actually likes the thing you want them to do.

Parenting: From A Child's Perspective

<u>You Are Not Your Child</u>

Point To Ponder: As A Parent, Not Only Do You Begin To Shape Your Child's View On Life, But You Also (To An Extent) Play A Role In Shaping Your Child's Fears.

Questions To Consider: Are You Parenting Your Younger Self Or Your Child?

Impact Of

Family

Dynamics

Parenting: From A Child's Perspective

Each family has a unique set of dynamics, which will impact our development, ideas, and ways of behaving as well as how we interact with others. Families show the child and gives guidance about personal values and social behavior through culture and beliefs. These values will predict how the child performs at home and other social settings such as school, church, or sporting activities. We gain our personality and our individuality through the family make up. Our family and closest people that are around will have an impact on how a child develops and behaves. All families are different, but every family provides the values and norms that a child develops through. The family provides the foundation for socialization, emotional stability, and cognitive and physical development. Children who grow up in healthy, stable, and loving families will have a greater chance at future success. The interaction of children with their families is key for physical and cognitive development. Families who participate in social activities, such as game playing, contribute to their child's long-term development, both physically and

Parenting: From A Child's Perspective

cognitively. Research indicates that siblings have a huge impact on a child's development. Siblings can be role models and the first influence on social interactions and competition. Sibling relationships are likely to last longer than any other relationship and plays a vital role in family life. The family is where the child is able to feel like his or her self. Within the family, feelings and thoughts should be expressed freely. Children are more likely to have trusting relationships with parents who are consistent and nurturing. This will lead to a number of positive developmental outcomes and children will be at lower risk for mental illness such as depression and anxiety. Abuse, neglect and trauma always take place in a social context. The impact of abuse is not limited to the person who has been abused. The same kind of constriction happens in families in which one person has been abused, whether or not the abuser is part of the family. The influences of family dynamics will of course vary from family to family, and will often include previous generations, as well as the current living generations. Social economic factors, class,

Parenting: From A Child's Perspective

culture and geographic location will also play key roles in how family dynamics are established, maintained and also fractured. Common factors that may influence the development of family dynamics are:

❖ The nature of your parent's relationship

❖ A parent who was absent for a period of your life.

❖ A Mix of Family Members (Aunts, Uncles, Cousins)

❖ External events

❖ Illness, Trauma, Death, Unemployment

❖ Dynamics Of Previous Generations.

❖ The Strictness Of Your Parents

❖ Types of Personalities In The Families

The word family is a single word with multiple meanings. It represents many different things, and holds within it a wide range of feelings, thoughts and ideas. Even where there has been little contact with a family, we will have all been influenced by the dynamics we experienced in our early lives. Our family dynamics

Parenting: From A Child's Perspective

impact on how we see ourselves in later life, influence our relationships, how we interact with the world as well as our well-being. However we personally define family, it is inherent that there will be complex feelings and issues held within the relationships in our familial circle. Parents make it your job to assess some of the dynamics in your family. What do you think was handed to you that you didn't like? Do you do those same things? Whatever you needed while you were younger try to TEACH your child, don't always just give it.

Parenting: From A Child's Perspective

Impact Of Family Dynamics On Children

Point To Ponder: You Have The Ability To Hurt Or Benefit Not Only The Parenting Of Your Child, But Also To An Extent Of The Way Your Grandchildren Are Treated.

Questions To Consider: Are There Some Characteristics You Have That Are Negative As A Parent, That Your Parents Had?

Go The

Distance

Parenting: From A Child's Perspective

When I was in first grade, I didn't really like sitting down for too long, nor did I seem interested in the work. As time went on, my teacher got worried for me and not only was she worried, she told my parents that I had ADD & ADHD. She told my parents my attention span was short and I never appeared to care about the work. She even offered a doctor for me to go to so I could be taken care of correctly. The great parents that I have never take anything of that nature without first seeing what can be done. My mom took me to get tested at the best school in Delaware at the time. At that school they gave me what I thought was a regular test that I have been taking at my old school, but in reality it was a placement test. During that test, the teacher said I was allowed to sing, dance, and/or listen to music to just be completely free of anything else. Days later, the results finally came in and my teacher was right, I wasn't interested in first grade work. I had tested in every area for 3rd grade and above, even being asked if I wanted to

Parenting: From A Child's Perspective

skip a grade. My parents taking the option to not listen to my teacher and go the distance in this situation, instead of just taking it for what it was is extremely important for how I live my life today. It doesn't have to be this situation, it can be any situation that requires more from you as a parent to get to the bottom of it and do as much as you can for your children. That is what going the distance means. Always seek the truth and always take action before making life changing decisions.

Parenting: From A Child's Perspective

Go The Distance

Point To Ponder: There Are Life Changing Things That Come Up, You Can Take Them For Face Value Or Get To The Root.

Questions To Consider: What Are Some Ways Right Now You Can Go The Distance For Your Child?

Use

Impactful

Discipline

Parenting: From A Child's Perspective

Discipline: the practice of training people to obey rules or a code of behavior, using punishment to correct disobedience. The purpose of discipline is changed behavior, so it would only make sense that the discipline is actually impacting the intended person. If there is a disobedient child that hates going outside, what sense would it make to take his privilege to go outside. The difference you want to see has to come from something that will make a difference in the child's everyday life. Punishment doesn't always have to be physical. Punishment can be from taking something away, and even sometimes letting your child "bump their head" so they can see for themselves what you were trying to do for them the whole time. Are you getting the desired results from your current ways of discipline? You might want to review your avenues of discipline to make sure it impacts your child and creates the positive change as intended.

Parenting: From A Child's Perspective

<u>Use Impactful Discipline</u>

Point To Ponder: Discipline Is Supposed To Correct Behavior, Make Sure That This Remains The Focus Regardless Of How It Is Done.

Question To Consider: Are Your Children Responding To Your Current Way(s) Of Discipline?

BE

THERE

Parenting: From A Child's Perspective

One thing that cannot be replaced is being there for your child. I polled 100 students on a college campus to see if children preferred to win or win with their parents there during an event, game, or spelling bee, etc. to see the impact of their parents support. There was a variety of parents included in the survey; some children had both parents, some had one mom, some had one dad. There were divorced parents, there were some still married. I asked the students would you rather win at something you do or would you rather win at something you do and have your parents be in attendance. After fully tallying the survey, 100 out of 100 college students, all with different parenting situations all said that they would rather have their parents **be there** in attendance for support. Being there is not a small difference whatsoever, it is a huge difference to children to know that our parents are there for us. That also goes for negative and down times as well where we need our parents there to pick us up, not just in good moments. In

Parenting: From A Child's Perspective

9th Grade When I Was 14(I'm 22 Now), my school just as every other school was having basketball tryouts. Two weeks before tryouts, we had an open gym for our school where everybody could come and play. During that open gym oooooooooo man I never played that well in my entire life. I didn't even know I was that good, I was shocking myself. I was doing everything right and making all my shots. Even my last shot of the day, a smooth stepback three pointer I had been working on at the gym the entire past two weeks prior went right through the net. I felt good about myself as well as others who played around me, friends coming up to me telling me I played well. You couldn't tell me anything that day, I was on top of the world. Fast forward two weeks, it was the first day of tryouts and my energy was up, I felt amazing we got started on shooting drills and I couldn't make a shot. I couldn't throw a basketball in a lake if I had tried on this day to be honest with you. After that we had played 3 on 3 and 5 on 5, and the

Parenting: From A Child's Perspective

same thing again was taking place. I couldn't make a shot, I was turning the ball over and my frustrations began to show. I ended up being beyond hard on myself and that only made me play worse, my mindset was out of it and that is the worst place to be. The second day wasn't a repeat of the first I did okay, but I wasn't sure if it was enough. A few days later the list of people who made the team came out and my name wasn't on there. Looking back I needed to work harder, have a better mindset going in as well as just realize I simply wasn't good enough. It is easy to take accountability and ownership now but in that moment I hated everything and everybody. I felt bad and sick to my stomach after finding out I didn't make it. I was so mad to the point that I had tears flowing out of anger. I called my dad and told him what happened, he came to the school and picked me up and immediately took me to see the movie Unstoppable with Denzel Washington. We watched it, and my dad just continued to tell me that I was unstoppable and walked through the whole process with me. Not only did he take me to the movies but he also had a conversation with me about the importance of self-reflecting on what I could have done better and working hard. My father being there in that moment is monumental for me, that moment also helped mold me and create the work ethic I now have today. There are people who have nobody in their lives to be there for them in these type of situations, and I myself can only imagine where I would be today if my father.

Parenting: From A Child's Perspective

<u>BE THERE</u>

Point To Ponder: Think Of Someone You Supported And Ask Yourself How That Made Them Feel.

Questions To Consider: What Are Some Different Ways You Can Be There For Those Around You?

Instill A High Level Of Self-Esteem In Your Child

Parenting: From A Child's Perspective

Having a high level of self-esteem starts at home and starts the moment children are born. You should go out your way in creating children who feel good about themselves, and giving them the confidence to do new things. Instilling a high level of self-esteem protects your child and helping them have mental toughness will do more than you can imagine. Having a high self-esteem even helps kids cope with mistakes. It helps kids try again, even if they fail at first. As a result, self-esteem helps kids do better at school, at home, and with friends. Kids with low self-esteem feel unsure of themselves. If they think others won't accept them, they may not join in. They may let others treat them poorly. They may have a hard time standing up for themselves. They may give up easily, or not try at all. Kids with low self-esteem find it hard to cope when they make a mistake, lose, or fail. As a result, they may not do as well as they could. Self-esteem can start as previously mentioned as early as babyhood. It develops slowly but surely over time. It can start literally just because a child feels safe, loved, and accepted at home. It can start

Parenting: From A Child's Perspective

when a baby gets positive attention and loving care. As babies become toddlers and young children, they're able to do some things all by themselves. They feel good about themselves when they can use their new skills. Their self-esteem grows when parents pay attention, let a child try, give smiles, and show they're proud. As kids grow, self-esteem can grow too. Any time kids try things, do things, and learn things can be a chance for self-esteem to grow. Ways self-esteem raises in young children are:

❖ Making Progress Toward A Goal

❖ Learning Things At School

❖ Make Friends and get along

❖ Learn How To Do New Things & Gaining Skill Sets Helping Others

❖ Being Acknowledged For Achievement Of Some Sort

❖ Having To Work For Something And Getting It

❖ Doing Things They're Good At

❖ Included

❖ Feeling Understood

Parenting: From A Child's Perspective

❖   get a prize or a good grade they know they've earned

When kids have high self-esteem, they are more confident as well as feel more capable. Jumping back to one of the chapter titles earlier in the book to say again, *Every Child Is Different.* Self-esteem may come easier to some kids than others. Some kids face things that can lower their self-esteem. But even if a child's self-esteem is low, it *can* be raised. There are things parents can to help kids feel good about themselves like :

Help your child learn to do things. At every age, there are new things for kids to learn. Even during babyhood, learning to hold a cup or take first steps sparks a sense of mastery and delight. As your child grows, things like learning to dress, read, or ride a bike are chances for self-esteem to grow.

When teaching kids how to do things, show and help them at first. Then let them do what they can, even if they make mistakes. Be sure your child gets a chance to learn, try, and feel proud. Don't make new challenges too easy — or too hard.

Be a good role model. When you put effort into everyday tasks, you're setting a good example. Your child learns to put effort into doing homework, cleaning up toys, or making the bed.

Modeling the right attitude counts too. When you do tasks cheerfully or at least without grumbling or complaining, you teach your child to do the same. When you avoid rushing through chores and take pride in a job well done, you teach your child to do that too.

Don't talk down on your children. The messages kids hear about themselves from others easily translate into how they feel about themselves. A parents insults are much more harmful than a random person saying something, on top of that it is not motivating at all. When kids hear negative messages about themselves, it harms their self-esteem. Correct kids with patience.

Parenting: From A Child's Perspective

Focus on what you want them to do next time. When needed, show them how.

Focus on your child's strengths. Pay attention to what your child does well and enjoys. Make sure your child has chances to develop these strengths. Focus more on strengths than weaknesses if you want to help kids feel good about themselves. This improves behavior too.

Parenting: From A Child's Perspective

High Self-Esteem Children:

❖   Feel Liked & Accepted ~ Or Sometimes Have No Care

❖   Feel Confident

❖   Feel Proud Of Their Abilities

❖   Think Good Thoughts & Have Positive Self-Talk

❖   Believe In Themselves

Kids With Low Self-Esteem:

❖   Are Very Self-Critical & Hard On Themselves

❖   Feel As If They're Not Enough

❖   Think About Failing Before Trying

❖   Lack Confidence

❖   Doubt Themselves

Parenting: From A Child's Perspective

Instill A High Level Of Self-Esteem In Your Child

Point To Ponder: Suicide Is Increasing By Ridiculous Numbers, Along With Anxiety, Depression, Disorders... Why Not Already Make Your Child Have A Strong Mind Early On.

Questions To Consider: You Can Take The Time To Instill A High Level of Self-Esteem In Your Child, Or You Can Let The World Do It.. It Doesn't Always Turn Out How You Want.

Hindering

Parent

Behaviors

Parenting: From A Child's Perspective

Parents, in most situations, love and want to protect their children in every way possible. There are also instances where that love and protection is actually hurting the life of the child. Before saying anything else, let me get straight into explaining what I mean. Parents don't always let their children experience taking chances. We live in a society that has dangers at every turn and sees failure as a bad thing. The "safety before anything else" mindset forces some parents fear of losing their children, so they do anything and everything to protect them. Don't get me wrong at all, it is a parents job after all, but sometimes it is done to the extent where it has a reverse impact. Children need to fall or fail a few times to learn and understand that failure happens and it is normal. Regardless of how much love and protection a parent gives, it is impossible to protect your child from everything, so you are better off preparing them for it. There will be times where we as children need to feel that pain or go through certain

Parenting: From A Child's Perspective

experiences to grow. Leading us into the next point, rescuing the child too quickly can also hinder them. In this generation, society has become more sensitive than in the past. The change is somewhat due to children being saved from every situation early on by their parents. When parents step in too quickly, it removes the need for the child to deal with hardships and solve problems. In the moment, it may seem like you are saving your child, but in reality you are hurting them on the back end. It's parenting for the short-term, and with that it also removes the desire for your child to do for self outside the home. Eventually children will get used to someone rescuing them; which in reality sets them up for failure because that is not how the real world works, whatsoever. Let your kids mess up sometimes and show them how to learn from their mistakes so they can grow wiser and become stronger. You want your parenting to connect with reality, and that leads to next point of giving praise too easily. Often times in today's society

Parenting: From A Child's Perspective

you see things like "everybody must be able to play" or "everybody is a winner," but it is a facade. Again, this is diservicing the child's long term life for short term happiness. Trying to use this mentality only makes children feel special temporarily, but has many consequences. The next point to be made is sometimes parents let guilt get in the way of proper parenting. If your child does wrong and needs to be disciplined, don't go out your way to comfort them directly or take it back. Your child does not have to love you every second of the day. Your kids will get over the moment and even thank you later in life. Telling your children no or not right now and letting them fight for what they really value and want will benefit them. Giving in to your children because they are upset at you or because they keep asking will again cripple them in the long run. This is unrealistic in the real world and misses a parenting opportunity to show kids that you have to deal with reality as well as the decisions you make. In addition, make sure your relationship with your child is not built on material things; materialism often takes precedent and kids will no longer be able to experience deep-rooted motivation or unconditional love. Speaking of love, the next point is a key component of that: transparency. Sometimes as children our parents haven't shared their past mistakes or experiences with us. To some children that causes them to try to keep the "perfect image" around you and could lead to your child not sharing their mistakes. Expecting your kids to be great is healthy, but expecting them to be perfect will backfire. Teach your kids that it's okay to fail. Kids who strive to become the best version of *themselves*, rather than the best at everything, won't make their self-worth dependent upon how they measure up to others. Letting children know where you went wrong, messed up in the past, and in the now can give them wisdom and possibly prevent them from making those same mistakes. Not only that, but it also shows your child it is okay to speak

Parenting: From A Child's Perspective

on wrongdoings and to be transparent with you in return. Share with them similar mistakes you made when you were younger in a way that helps them learn and move forward in a positive direction. Teach children to be accountable as well as prepare to face problems and the consequences of their decisions. Understand that there are many different influences on kids lives, but parents must be the best influence. A great way to be a great influence is to be a great example. Sometimes that example is messed up by the next point: not practicing what you preach as a parent. As parents, it is your responsibility to model the life you want your children to live. Not meaning copying your occupation, but by leading a life of character, being dependable, and accountable for your words and actions. Since parents are the head of the house, when they follow up their words with their actions they create a standard. Parents, also watch yourself in the little choices that others may notice, because your kids will notice too. If you don't take shortcuts, most likely your children will know it's not acceptable for them to either. Parents sometimes say, act, or do things that they might not necessarily think is a big deal or a problem at all, but you would be surprised as to how that can hurt a child. One thing you don't want to do is compare your child to other children, unless of course you are trying to make your child feel inferior. If you can, stay far from pointless judgements and comparisons. Believe in your child, and your child's individuality. Cheering your children up EVERY TIME they're sad and calming them down EVERY TIME they're upset means you are take responsibility for regulating their emotions. You have to let children gain emotional competence so they can learn to manage their own feelings. Teach your child healthy ways to cope with their emotions, and to not let them give control of those emotions to other things or people.

Parenting: From A Child's Perspective

<u>Hindering Parent Behaviors</u>

Point To Ponder: Prepare Your Child For The Reality Of Life, Don't Try To Shield Them From It.

Question To Consider: Are You (THE PARENT) Sacrificing Your Child's Long-Term Growth For Short-Term Comfort?

ENDING

THOUGHTS

& IDEAS

Parenting: From A Child's Perspective

❖   Try To Understand Your CHILD'S Love Language

❖   Never Fake Praise Or Show Undeserving Praise In Bad Moments

❖   Don't Stop Children From Voicing Their Opinions (Respectfully)

❖   Don't Throw Life Altering Decisions On Children Too Early

❖   Don't "Act" Like Perfect Parents

➢   Let your children see the what it takes, don't try to hide what really takes place and goes on

❖   Never Condone Victim Mentality

❖   Don't Have Your Children Thinking That Life Revolves Around Them

➢   Making kids the center of the universe will only lead to them growing up thinking everyone should cater to them. You know and I know self-absorbed, entitled adults don't get very far in life.

Parenting: From A Child's Perspective

❖ Don't Allow Fear To Dictate Your Parenting Choices

❖ You SHOULD Have Life Insurance For Your Family

❖ You SHOULD Speed Up Your Child's Learning & Importance Of Self Education

❖ Financial Literacy SHOULD Be Taught In The Home

➢ Debt, Credit, Wealth, Investing ETC. Is Not Taught At School

❖ Prepare Your Child More Than Prevent, There Will Be A Time You Have To Let The Child Go

❖ Have Regular Conversations With Your Children

❖ Establish The Friend/Parent Balance Early On

❖ You Are The First Role Model

❖ You Have The Power To Shift Your Family Dynamics

<u>Reason For Writing</u>

After writing my first book *EVOLVE: Eliminating Negative Thinking & Empowering Your Thoughts,* and impacting people's lives as far as mental health, I wanted to further go in to executing my purpose. One of my purposes is to impact and empower other people, even more specifically to impact the next generation. I couldn't think of a better way to impact the next generation than to impact the people who play a big role in shaping the next generation: *PARENTS.* This book isn't to bash parents in any way whatsoever, but to offer a new **perspective** that most parents may not have experienced or have had to think about. Parenting is one of the hardest jobs and the world and one of the few jobs where you can do everything right and the child still not turn out right. Whether because of outside influences, what they choose to value but on the other hand parents have to realize the child's actions are NOT ALWAYS a result of their parenting. With this book I

Parenting: From A Child's Perspective

just wanted to equip parents with more ideas and ways to go about things to continue to strive to be the best parents they can be.

<u>ABOUT THE AUTHOR</u>

- ❖ Author of 2 Books
- ❖ Purpose In Life Are To Empower & Educate People Mentally & Financially, As Well As To Change Lives
- ❖ Keynote Speaker On A Variety of Topics Networking, Value, Transitioning Etc.
- ❖ Founder & Facilitator of Operation Overhaul, Will Soon Be Turned Into A Non-Profit
- ❖ Founder & Facilitator of Mental Health & Generational Wealth Workshops
- ❖ All About Giving Back & Educating Those Who Seek To Be Educated
- ❖ Forex Trader
- ❖ Servant Leader In The Community
- ❖ Revolves Life Around Impacting Others
- ❖ Life & Health Insurance Licensed
- ❖ ONLY A Senior In College ~ 1ST HBCU Lincoln University

Parenting: From A Child's Perspective

❖ Has many projects releasing over the next few months as well as Creator & Host of *Power In Perspectives*

❖ www.CEOMillsINC.com is his website for all news, updates, ventures, releases and store to purchase both books

Parenting: From A Child's Perspective

CONTACT

EMAIL: miciah.mills@lincoln.edu

PHONE: 302-750-3430

WEBSITE: www.ceomillsinc.com

FEEDBACK

THANK YOU FOR READING THIS BOOK, I GREATLY APPRECIATE IT. IF YOU COULD TAKE THE TIME TO INFORM ME & GIVE ME FEEDBACK VIA EMAIL IT WORLD MEAN A LOT TO ME. FOR FUTURE READER'S SAKE, BE COMPLETELY HONEST WITH ME, IT WILL LET ME MAKE THE BOOK BETTER AS TIME GOES ON.

34058229R00040

Made in the USA
Middletown, DE
22 January 2019